to Transform
Your Leadership

com
mon
GREATNESS

Quick Start
Guide

MARK MILLER & RANDY GRAVITT

Printed in the United States of America

Design and Layout by Lindsay Miller

Printing Information
Bennett Graphics
125 Royal Woods Court, Suite 100
Tucker, GA 30084
Tel: (770) 723-1192
www.BennettGraphics.com

ISBN 979-8-9897448-0-0

Table of Contents

Welcome

FOR A FULL OVERVIEW OF *UNCOMMON GREATNESS*, PLEASE REFERENCE THE *UNCOMMON GREATNESS* BOOK AND FIELD GUIDE, AVAILABLE AT LEADEVERYDAY.COM.

Welcome to the *Uncommon Greatness Quick Start Guide*!

Let's start with the obvious question: What does it mean to achieve uncommon greatness?

To answer this, we'll first offer a deeply held belief: you were created for greatness. We firmly believe every human being contains within them the potential to be great.

Now, what does it mean to be uncommon?

Defining uncommon greatness begins with defining common greatness. Common greatness is fleeting, focused on the achievement, and centered on the achiever. It is typically acknowledged on a public scale and celebrated widely, so that it emboldens the individual and exalts personal excellence.

Uncommon greatness is less about the self, and all about how you help others, your organization, and—ultimately—your world be great. It is enduring and focused on the contribution. It is rarely recognized publicly—and may go unnoticed entirely—but it empowers others and lifts those around you to new levels of excellence.

In this resource, we will dive into the Five Fundamentals and their subsequent strategies and tactics to pave the path to uncommon greatness. If you're familiar with our resources, many may sound familiar. Ultimately, they reflect a combination of the best practices regarding leadership skill and character identified in *The Secret: What Great Leaders Know and Do*, and *The Heart of Leadership*.

We hope this Quick Start Guide will supplement the book even further, as you unpack the team discussion topics and activation ideas. The world needs you. Now, be great!

MARK MILLER AND RANDY GRAVITT

See the Future

SECTION ONE

Whether seeing the potential in a developing leader, envisioning the final product at the start of a brainstorm, or having the intuition to move into an emerging market, leaders see things before others do. And, in doing so, leaders who See the Future possess a noticeable advantage over the competition.

However, seeing around the corner is not all there is to being an effective leader. The best ones understand the need to remember the past, learning from challenges and reviewing achievements and setbacks as they move forward. At the same time, great leaders know how to remain grounded in reality, realizing they must start where they are before expecting to climb some aspirational mountain. Once they gain a proper perspective, true leaders have an ability to dream of a better place: one full of possibilities, worth changing for, and where others will want to follow.

Leaders see things
before others do.

Remember the Past

Seeing the future starts with a trip to the past—albeit, not for long.

To **Remember the Past**, start with listening to the founders. Those who gave life to your organization likely saw something, and revisiting their aims, successes, and setbacks can help your own vision of the future.

Then, think about the time since your organization's founding until more recently. Your awareness of past challenges, milestones, and what patterns exist is critical as you look toward the future.

And, finally, the best leaders learn in real time and identify what they're doing today to make tomorrow better, often best done through After-Action Reviews.

If you're ready to see the future, start by remembering the past!

Question to Consider

What lessons from your company's history are important to consider as you plan for the future?

THE BEST LEADERS LEARN FROM THE PAST BUT DON'T LIVE THERE.

LEARNING FROM TODAY MAKES TOMORROW BETTER.

LESSONS FROM THE PAST ARE WAITING TO GUIDE YOUR PATH FORWARD.

ACTIVATION IDEAS TO

Remember the Past

☐ **Listen to the Founders**

IN YOUR SHOES: Imagine the founders of your company are in your role today. What do you believe they'd do differently, if leading the company as it currently stands? Create a 10-year vision based on the founders' hypothetical perspective.

DATE COMPLETED: _____

☐ **Understand Past Challenges**

TOP TEN: Make a list of the top ten challenges in your company's history. (This can be sourced by speaking to those who worked in the "early days" or by scanning the archives.) For each, ask yourself: Why did we encounter this problem? What was our response? What could have prevented this problem? What did we learn?

DATE COMPLETED: _____

☐ Create a Milestones Map

DRAW IT OUT: Create a timeline of noteworthy milestones in your organization's history. Make time on your calendar to focus solely on determining what you can learn from the patterns in your past.

DATE COMPLETED: _____

☐ Do After-Action Reviews:

LEARN IT: Free resources—video series, blogs, PDFs, eBooks, and more—all exist focused on how to do an effective AAR. Gather your team for a lunch & learn focused on learning the best practices before you ever implement the process.

DATE COMPLETED: _____

Remain
Grounded

I f leaders expect to remain effective, they must **Remain Grounded** in reality.

This starts with a leader who looks in the mirror and admits there is progress to be made. They maintain a customer bias, in hopes of gaining a sense of how to improve. Better yet, they go and see for themselves, observing day-to-day functions of their team to witness how things are really going. Additionally, reality can be discerned from trusted counsel: by listening broadly and proactively and inviting contrarian points of view to provide a level of honesty.

If great leaders want to see the future and get there, they know it is crucial to embrace their current reality as a starting point.

Question to Consider

When was the last time you invested a day to assess your current reality?

TRUTH IS A LEADER'S BEST FRIEND.

YOU HAVE TO START WHERE YOU ARE, BUT YOU DON'T HAVE TO STAY THERE.

LEADERS MUST LISTEN BROADLY AND PROACTIVELY TO REMAIN GROUNDED IN REALITY.

Remain Grounded

☐ Maintain a Customer Bias

FOCUS GROUP: Organize a pilot focus group to listen to your customers. (If you have the resources, we recommend hiring a professional.) Ensure you ask open-ended questions, avoid defensiveness, and take good notes.

DATE COMPLETED: _____

☐ Go and See for Yourself

FIELD TRIP: When was the last time you went out "to the field?" Put it on your calendar. Consider going unannounced—or even anonymously, if possible—and stay long enough to see things, hear things, and have people open up to you on issues they're facing.

DATE COMPLETED: _____

☐ Voice List

VOICE LIST: Make a strategic listening plan for the next twelve months by listing all of the audiences you would like to engage with in a typical year. How often will you plan to engage with each? Start setting up meetings and determining how you will stick to your plan.

DATE COMPLETED: _____

☐ Invite Contrarian Views

ASSIGNED DEBATE: In order to set the expectation that contrarian views are not only welcomed but needed, perform an exercise where employees are asked to argue a point different from their own. Assign contrarian views and have them attempt to make the case for why it is the preferred choice of action.

DATE COMPLETED: _____

Dare
to Dream

By definition, seeing the future requires dreaming.

The first way in which leaders Dare to Dream is by elongating their perspective. They avoid engrossing themselves in the firefighting of the day-to-day business and think long-term about how decisions will affect the future and what that far-off future looks like.

Once they're on the path to dreaming big, visionary leaders consider the consequences of not taking the journey.

And, finally, the best leaders wake up thinking, "What if?" After all, many ideas lead to better ideas.

If you intend to be a visionary leader who sees the future and mobilizes others to join you, you must dare to dream—and dream big!

Question to Consider

Why is it so important
for a leader to dream?

**LEADERS ARE THE ARCHITECTS
OF THE FUTURE.**

MANY IDEAS LEAD TO BETTER IDEAS.

THE BEST LEADERS ASK, "WHAT IF?"

Dare to Dream

☐ Elongate Your Perspective

FUTURE METRICS: Imagine you are looking at the health indicators of your organization a decade or two from now. What metrics would you measure? With these metrics in mind, what can you do today to nudge them in the right direction?

DATE COMPLETED: _____

☐ Identify the Risks of Not Changing

CONSIDER COMPLACENCY: Allow yourself to imagine the negative possibilities of what your future looks like if you remain complacent with the status quo. Discuss this unfavorable future with others, and how you can act to avoid it becoming your reality.

DATE COMPLETED: _____

☐ Imagine the Possibilities

"WHAT IF" LIST: Start a "What If" list. Every day, add at least one idea to your list. (Think, "What if we changed _____? What if we started _____? What if we tried _____?")

DATE COMPLETED: _____

Engage and Develop Others

SECTION TWO

Vision alone will not be enough to create greatness. After all, if your dreams are big enough, you will need a team to help you realize them.

However, no team drifts to greatness, either. They must be led there, and great leaders know that their role to Engage and Develop Others is their highest priority.

Engagement of people begins with a foundation of trust: creating a culture where employees feel psychologically safe to show up and do their best.

Once this foundation is established, the best leaders help promote greatness in others by helping people grow, building genuine community, and casting dynamic, consistent, and crystal-clear vision.

After all, the development of people provides the foundation for future success, which is far too important to be left to chance. If this is a new idea for you, you are in for a real treat—a life-changing, leadership-altering treat!

No team drifts to greatness. They must be led there.

Build Trust

Every leader wants—and needs—trust. A workplace with a lack of trust will have compliant followers, at best, and the chasm between compliant and committed followers is vast: one is destined for mediocrity while the other can sustain levels of elite performance.

To Build Trust, leaders need to create a safe workplace—physically and psychologically. This involves building diverse teams that honor all voices, focusing on problems over people, and facilitating open dialogue.

Second, leaders need to watch their words, knowing that their voice is the loudest voice in the organization.

Lastly, building trust starts with trusting people. It sounds obvious, but challenge yourself to trust others, and watch as you expand your leadership capacity.

Question to Consider

How could you trust more?
Where are you refusing
to relinquish control?

Things to Remember

**TRUST LEADS TO COMMITTED—
RATHER THAN COMPLIANT—FOLLOWERS.**

**TRUST MUST BE EARNED
THROUGH STRATEGIC EFFORTS.**

**TRUSTING OTHERS EXPANDS
LEADERSHIP CAPACITY.**

Build Trust

☐ Create Safety

FACILITATOR DESIGNATOR: Ensure each meeting held has a designated facilitator, whose goal is to remove barriers for participation and is a steward of psychological safety.

DATE COMPLETED: _____

☐ Watch Your Words

KILLER PHRASES: Make a list of phrases you believe are impeding trust, innovation, and risk-taking in your organization. (Examples in the book include phrases such as "That will never work," and "Are you kidding me?") Ask those closest to you for words they hear you repeatedly say that may fall into this category. Ban all "Killer Phrases" from your vocabulary.

DATE COMPLETED: _____

☐ Trust Others

TRUST SCORE: Make a list of your direct reports, and score each one on a scale of 1 ("I don't trust this person") to 5 ("I trust this person completely"). Start at the bottom and consider what actions you could take over the coming weeks to begin trusting them more.

DATE COMPLETED: _____

Help
People
Grow

Your capacity to grow determines your capacity to lead.

It's a critical concept we've repeated in our resources over the years. However, when it comes to engaging and developing others, we have an additional note: your capacity to grow others determines your capacity for greatness.

To Help People Grow, leaders must focus on championing individual growth by meeting people where they are and recognizing their unique learning styles and career objectives, recognizing and rewarding growth as it happens, and providing the resources to fuel growth.

The best thing you can do for those you lead is to create a culture where the people, projects, and organization are growing toward greatness. It's time to grow!

Question to Consider

How much time do you spend developing those you lead?

THE BEST LEADERS EXPECT EVERYONE TO GROW.

YOUR CAPACITY TO GROW DETERMINES YOUR CAPACITY TO LEAD.

GROWING LEADERS GROW ORGANIZATIONS.

ACTIVATION IDEAS TO

Help
People Grow

☐ **Champion Individual Support**

SHARE GROWTH: Whenever you read, watch videos online, or run across meaningful content, send out a summary or link to your team members who you think would personally benefit from the particular content. Discuss the key points at your next 1:1 meeting.

DATE COMPLETED: _____

☐ **Recognize Growth**

REWARD IDEAS: Meet with members of your team and ask them to tell you about the best recognition they've ever received. Take good notes to form a collection of ideas.

DATE COMPLETED: _____

☐ Provide Resources

ASK THE SOURCE: This coming month, set up meetings with members of your team. Reiterate your desire to help them grow, and ask what resources they believe would be most helpful.

DATE COMPLETED: _____

Build Genuine Community

Any employee knows what it means to feel engaged at work. Fewer, unfortunately, can say they truly experience it.

This is because a key part of engaging and developing others requires Building Genuine Community—an environment where people genuinely care about one another. Community must be cultivated over time and a leader sets the strategy to make it so.

This strategy requires a focus on diversity so everyone feels like he or she belongs, promoting a deep knowledge of one another, and celebrating often: individual milestones, personal growth, and the achievement of dreams both within the office and beyond.

Skills and talent are taken to a higher level when there is a sense of community!

Question to Consider

Is your workplace a place where people unconditionally serve one another?

Things to Remember

COMMUNITY IS A PLACE WHERE PEOPLE GENUINELY CARE ABOUT AND SERVE ONE ANOTHER.

LEADERS SET A STRATEGY TO CULTIVATE COMMUNITY.

A SENSE OF COMMUNITY CATAPULTS TEAMS TO GREATNESS.

Build Genuine Community

☐ Set the Strategy

CALENDAR BLOCK: Is there time on your calendar devoted to strategizing on how to build community? In *Smart Leadership*, we called this time "margin." Time meant to think, where you are not encumbered by the busyness of the business. Schedule time now in the next week for your strategy brainstorm.

DATE COMPLETED: _____

☐ Value Diversity

BASEBALL ANALYSIS: In the book, we discussed diversity in terms of a baseball team. Imagine a baseball team was fielded with nine second basemen. Now, analyze your own team: Where is there room for growth in terms of diversity?

DATE COMPLETED: _____

☐ Promote Deep Knowledge of Others

MEETING QUESTIONS: At each meeting with your team, try asking casual, non-work-related questions to promote a sense of knowing. These may feel trivial, but remember: community is cumulative.

DATE COMPLETED: _____

☐ Celebrate Often

CELEBRATION CALENDAR: As the leader, keep a calendar of worthy celebrations of each member of your team: birthdays, work anniversaries, and even personal milestones—college graduations or their wedding date! Find a small way to celebrate often on an individual level.

DATE COMPLETED: _____

Cast Dynamic Vision

Building trust, helping people grow, and building community are three of the pillars needed to engage and develop your people. However, none of these alone will lead to the realization of dreams. What truly leads to engagement, execution, and greatness is rallying people behind an inspiring movement. Ultimately, it is the responsibility of the leader to Cast Dynamic Vision.

As you think about your vision, ask yourself: Is it clear? Is it succinct? Is it repeated often? Is it said in a way that everyone can understand?

When leaders cast their vision succinctly, frequently, and in ways that appeal to the different learning styles of their people, they'll find themselves surrounded by those who believe in them and the cause they are pursuing.

Question to Consider

Where are there opportunities to cast vision more often?

COMMITMENT TO A VISION IS KEY TO ENGAGEMENT.

THE VISION MUST BE CLEAR, SIMPLE, AND REPEATABLE.

LEADERS MUST CAST VISION IN WAYS TO APPEAL TO VARIOUS LEARNING STYLES.

Cast Dynamic Vision

☐ **Say It Succinctly**

ORGANIZATIONAL INDEX: Pass out index cards to ten people across your entire organization and ask them to write down your organization's vision. Are all of their answers the same? If not, there may be a lack of clarity or succinctness.

DATE COMPLETED: _____

☐ **Say It Again**

MEMORY JOG: Review your calendar for the past month to jog your memory as you ask yourself, "How many times did I talk about the vision?" Accept the challenge to talk about the vision in some shape or form every day, multiple times per day.

DATE COMPLETED: _____

☐ **Say It Differently**

TEAM ASSESSMENT: Schedule a meeting with your team where you review Gardner's eight intelligences, outlined in *Uncommon Greatness*. Have each team member discuss which style of learning they think they primarily identify with. Keep a list of this information to reference when communicating important items going forward.

DATE COMPLETED: _____

Reinvent Continuously

SECTION THREE

Leaders who believe the successes of today will serve them to win tomorrow will find themselves quickly behind the curve. They know that the only way to chase greatness for the long haul is to Reinvent Continuously.

This starts by thinking differently. If we want to reach our preferred future, we must go against our natural inclination to choose the tried-and-true and learn to be comfortable being uncomfortable.

On top of thinking differently, reinventing also involves creativity. Leaders flex this creativity muscle by expanding their worlds, escaping the known, and training their brains to think outside the box.

Beyond thinking and dreaming, at some point, leaders will be required to act. Leaders must act strategically by thinking big picture, reflecting often, and rethinking their processes, people, and structure.

Great leaders know that change is the only inevitable factor in today's environment, and they face it head-on, recognizing that progress is always preceded by change.

Wise leaders learn
to be comfortable
being uncomfortable.

Think Different

A big part of leaders seeing the unseen and a bigger part of reinventing continuously requires leaders to Think Different.

This thinking starts with investing the time. "Eureka" moments are often depicted as just that: moments. However, truly great ideas had likely been simmering for weeks, months, or even years.

Once leaders have devoted time to thinking, they must incorporate a few more tactics to do it well: they must consider contrarian points of view, ask more and better questions, and cultivate a broad network of resources to lean on.

Ultimately, the systems, work processes, and behaviors in your organization are perfectly aligned to the outcomes you are currently obtaining. If you want different results, start with different thinking.

Question to Consider

What daily practices are you currently undertaking to inspire you to think different?

WHAT GOT YOU HERE WON'T GET YOU THERE.

THE BEST LEADERS LOOK UNDER THE SURFACE OF A SITUATION.

DIFFERENT THINKING LEADS TO DIFFERENT RESULTS.

Think Different

☐ Invest the Time

TEAM BRAINSTORM: Think of a problem or topic you'd like to tackle with your team, and set up a ninety-minute brainstorming session (or longer!). Reference LeadEveryDay.com/uncommon for "Ten Tips for Brilliant Brainstorming."

DATE COMPLETED: _____

☐ Consider the Opposite

DIFFERENT CROWD: Identify three people who have a different worldview, different educational background, or work in a different industry than yours. Spend an hour with each of them and ask about their biggest current challenge and how they are addressing it.

DATE COMPLETED: _____

☐ Ask More and Better Questions

QUESTION COUNTER: Monitor the number of questions you ask in a typical day and work to increase your awareness and identify your tendencies. With your newfound awareness, experiment with asking more questions. See what happens.

DATE COMPLETED: _____

Cultivate Creativity

When you think of creativity, what comes to mind?

For many, the primary connotation is associated with art. However, an often-neglected meaning deals with thinking creatively.

Simply put, creative thinkers are able to generate multiple, viable options. They are able to consider obstacles and opportunities and come up with an array of possibilities for how to proceed. Given this definition, all leaders must work to Cultivate Creativity.

Fortunately, creativity is a muscle that can be strengthened. The best leaders exercise this muscle by expanding their worlds, seeking new and inspiring experiences beyond their comfort zones; escaping the known; and retraining the brain to escape the ruts it's innately carved to spark new pathways.

If you want to think different, you must think creative!

Question to Consider

What small thing can you do this week to change up your routine?

Things to Remember

CREATIVE THINKING IS THE ABILITY TO GENERATE VIABLE OPTIONS.

CREATIVITY CAN BE STRENGTHENED.

THINKING DIFFERENT REQUIRES THINKING CREATIVELY.

Cultivate Creativity

☐ Expand Your World

MONTHLY HIGHLIGHT: Is there something on your calendar in the next thirty days that might help you Expand Your World—a conversation, event, new restaurant, trip planned, or something else? If not, try adding something. If so, plan for the next thirty days so you have something monthly to look forward to.

DATE COMPLETED: _____

☐ Escape the Known

PAST PROBLEMS: Think of your biggest current challenge. What are you sure is true? Set that aside. If you couldn't continue with your current approach, how would you proceed? Devote time to thinking through and writing down your answers to these questions.

DATE COMPLETED: _____

☐ Train Your Brain

EXERCISE TIME: Buy a book containing techniques to spur your creative thinking. (For a list of resources, see the back of *Uncommon Greatness*.) Commit to trying a new technique every week for a month. Notice how each affects your proficiency and confidence.

DATE COMPLETED: _____

Act
Strategically

Reinventing—by definition—is a verb. Reinventing—like leadership—requires action. To reinvent continuously, leaders must **Act Strategically**.

Like a military leader, the best leaders have a strategy before ever stepping foot on the battlefield. They seek wise counsel and develop a plan that will provide their greatest probability of triumph. By thinking big picture and keeping the end result in mind, leaders know road bumps are not blockades, and strategic thinking is a never-ending practice to reach high-performance.

Leaders also evaluate their strategy by routinely looking in the mirror, evaluating what processes—and people—are and aren't working.

Great leaders are strategic over sporadic, knowing that unless they have a strategy for how to win, they never will.

Question to Consider

What must your team do to plan to win?

Act Strategically

☐ Think Big Picture

BIG ANSWERS: When you approach your next problem or opportunity, stop and ask yourself the following questions: What does long-term success look like on this issue? What does the bigger picture tell us about the problem at hand? What impact will our actions have on the broader organization?

DATE COMPLETED: _____

☐ Look in the Mirror

YEAR OF CHANGE: Do an audit of the last twelve months; how many of your working hours did you invest reinventing yourself? Now, look at the next twelve months; what are you willing to do differently to ensure you are investing adequately in your own reinvention?

DATE COMPLETED: _____

☐ Rethink the Processes

MAP IT: Identify one key work process where you believe you can either reduce cost, improve cycle time, reduce errors, or reduce redundancy. Map every step of the entire process, and then step back and look. Where can you see enhancements that can be made?

DATE COMPLETED: _____

☐ Check the Org Chart

STRUCTURE ANALYSIS: Sit with your key leaders and ask the question: What is the ideal structure to serve our customers over the next twelve months? When the structure is well-conceived, it will multiply the energy and effort of your team.

DATE COMPLETED: _____

Lead Purposeful Change

Leaders are paid to create progress; therefore, leaders must master the art of Leading Purposeful Change.

Leaders lead purposeful change first by maintaining dynamic awareness, knowing where, what, and who needs to change to make progress.

Next, they communicate change efforts tirelessly by communicating the vision, offering encouragement, and providing progress reports.

Leaders also must expand ownership for the change, knowing that for change to become embedded in the organization, everyone will need to buy in.

Once employees are committed, leaders will then provide support and iterate throughout the process, knowing the only thing guaranteed through a change effort is change itself.

If you plan on reaching your full potential, leading purposeful change will be one of your most important weapons.

Question to Consider

Why is it so important for leaders to be skilled at change management?

CHANGE IS INEVITABLE BUT HOW YOU LEAD IT IS A CHOICE.

CHANGE PRECEDES PROGRESS.

LEADERS HELP OTHERS NAVIGATE UNCERTAINTY.

Lead Purposeful Change

☐ Maintain Dynamic Awareness

IN THEIR SHOES: If your organization uses an employee survey of any type, take a copy and fill it out yourself as you think your employees will. When their results are tabulated compare their answers with what you thought they would say. How close are your projected responses to what they actually said?

DATE COMPLETED: _____

☐ Communicate Tirelessly

PARTY PLANNING: Ask employees now, "What ways would make you feel most appreciated when it's time to celebrate our progress in our change initiatives?" Keep a list of responses, and schedule celebrations when the opportunities arise.

DATE COMPLETED: _____

☐ Expand Ownership

DELEGATE AND DEPUTIZE: As the leader, you cannot lead every change effort. Make a list of the day-to-day issues associated with every change effort. Let employees know they all have your support, but assign ownership of each of these areas to a different point leader.

DATE COMPLETED: _____

☐ Provide Support

BE DIRECT: Identify a change initiative currently underway in your organization. Go to people from three different levels who are actively involved in implementation of the desired change, including someone from the frontlines. Ask them one question: What additional support do you need to make this change effort more successful?

DATE COMPLETED: _____

☐ Iterate Throughout the Process

THREE QUESTIONS: Look around your organization for a change project that is floundering or stuck. Talk to the leaders of this project and ask three questions: If you could do it all again, what would you do differently? Which of those insights could you apply now to restart this work? And, what support do you need to move forward?

DATE COMPLETED: _____

Value Results and Relationships

SECTION FOUR

Out of the five fundamentals, the ability of a leader to Value Results and Relationships might be the most challenging of all. This is because virtually every leader—99 percent, actually—has a natural bias.

Valuing both is critical as leaders set the example for their organization. People always watch the leader, and as you acknowledge and compensate for your natural bias, you will unknowingly pave the path for others to do the same.

Secondly, a leader who coaches their people for success will find both their results and relationships soaring.

And finally, as the leader, you also need to demonstrate care. Just like coaching for success, if you choose a culture of care, your relationships will thrive and results will be enhanced.

By setting the example, coaching for success, and demonstrating care, you position your team to optimize results while remembering people are how they will get there.

People always
watch the leader.

Set the Example

The tactics when it comes to **Setting the Example** form a three-step process. Each step must be completed before moving on to the next.

First, leaders must know the values. These may be labeled as such, or they may be answered by considering questions such as, "What commitments are you expecting people to make to your organization?" When you know the values, they will soon influence everything your organization does.

Once you know the values, you must begin the never-ending journey of sharing them.

Finally, leaders must walk the talk to engender trust, bolster credibility, and have a profound impact on culture.

Know the values, share the values, and live the values to set the example for an organization who values results and relationships.

Question to Consider

Am I walking the talk
in my leadership?

**A LEADER'S VOICE
IS THE LOUDEST VOICE.**

**VALUES WILL INFLUENCE EVERYTHING
YOUR ORGANIZATION DOES.**

**LEADERS KNOW THE VALUES, SHARE
THE VALUES, AND LIVE THE VALUES.**

Set the Example

☐ Know the Values

QUESTION REFLECTION: Take time reflecting on one of the three questions we posed regarding Knowing the Values in the book: What commitments are you expecting your team to make to you and the organization? How do you want people to work in your organization? And, what are the behavioral norms you want to see demonstrated as people do their jobs? Spend time writing down your answers.

DATE COMPLETED: _____

☐ Live the Values

GAP HONESTY: Ask trusted voices in your world to help you spot gaps between what you say is important (e.g., your values) and how you live. These can be tough but enlightening one-on-one conversations.

DATE COMPLETED: _____

☐ Share the Values

VALUE AMBASSADOR: Look at your calendar for the next thirty days. Identify at least a dozen specific opportunities to share one or more of your values. This could include one-on-one meetings, team meetings, new employee orientation, conversations with vendors, interviews with potential employees, encounters with your customers, an upcoming sales pitch, and more! Make it your mission to become the chief ambassador of your values.

DATE COMPLETED: _____

Coach for Success

Leaders hold many roles, perhaps none so important as serving as a coach.

Coaches have the power to unearth and ignite human potential, seeing things others cannot, offering a different set of knowledge and experience, and offering more encouragement than a peer might.

Leaders who embrace this role should start by providing situational coaching, knowing one-size-fits-all will never work. No matter the coaching style, they also must give great feedback—feedback that is honest, complete, timely, helpful, and actionable. And finally, coaches routinely praise progress, celebrating growth and acknowledging milestones.

As the leader, are you ready to don another hat as you Coach for Success? If so, you will quickly unlock untapped power of your people and your organization.

Question to Consider

How can you praise progress
in the next week for your team?

COACHES SEE THINGS OTHERS CANNOT.

**COACHING IS NOT A
ONE-SIZE-FITS-ALL ENDEAVOR.**

**A COACHING CULTURE CAN
UNLOCK UNTAPPED POTENTIAL.**

ACTIVATION IDEAS TO

Coach for Success

☐ Embrace the Role

NEW HAT: Update your job description—not literally, but in your mind. The next time you meet with a member of your team, imagine you are wearing a hat that says COACH on the front. See if this added role changes how you think about the conversation.

DATE COMPLETED: _____

☐ Provide Situational Coaching

COMPETENCY CURVE: The next time you are faced with an opportunity to coach someone, stop and consider where they are on their personal competency curve. They may have a decade of experience, with a high overall competency, but the task at hand may be totally new to them. Try adjusting your style to meet them where they are.

DATE COMPLETED: _____

☐ Give Great Feedback

PASS IT ON: To get an even better idea of what great feedback looks like, consider the best feedback you've ever received. How did it motivate, advise, or otherwise affect you? What can you learn to pay it forward?

DATE COMPLETED: _____

☐ Praise Progress

SIXFOLD PRAISE: Over the next week, look for at least half a dozen opportunities to praise the progress an individual has made on important work.

DATE COMPLETED: _____

Demonstrate Care

If you've ever added some greenery to your office or living space, you know that it isn't a lack of a green thumb that kills a plant; a lack of care does.

Like plants, people need consistent care to grow properly. As the leader, you have the power to keep them thriving.

The best leaders Demonstrate Care by practicing deep listening, keeping an ear out for both what is said and not said; by pursuing real relationships as they invest the time, remain curious and vulnerable, and stay in touch for the long term; and by letting people in, engaging on a personal level by integrating their personal and professional lives.

Do your people feel like you care? If you can help them flourish, your organization will as well.

Question to Consider

How do you know when someone really cares for you?

IN ORDER TO DEMONSTRATE CARE, FIRST YOU MUST CARE.

CARING STRENGTHENS RELATIONSHIPS AND RESULTS.

WHEN LEADERS CARE, EVERYONE BENEFITS.

Demonstrate Care

☐ **Practice Deep Listening**

OPEN DOOR HOURS: Create set hours each week where you are available to listen to your team members. Allow them time to share challenges with you, and be intentional about listening. Process possible solutions together. Give them permission to decide which are best.

DATE COMPLETED:

☐ **Pursue Real Relationships**

LOOK BACK: Identify a former coworker who you have lost touch with and attempt to jump-start that relationship. Don't stop there. Create your own plan for building genuine relationships with a few of your current coworkers.

DATE COMPLETED:

☐ **Engage at a Personal Level**

FAMILY TIES: At least one time each month, mail a handwritten note to the family of a coworker. Share what you appreciate most about this team member.

DATE COMPLETED: _____

Embody a Leader's Heart

For the past few decades, we've been advocating a picture of leadership that resembles the image of an iceberg. If you recall fifth-grade science class, you know that an iceberg only shows about 10 percent of its vastness above the water line. The same is true of leadership: the 10 percent visible above the surface represents leadership skills—the other four fundamentals outlined in this resource. The 90 percent below the surface represents leadership character. The truth is, if your heart is not right, no one cares about your skills. The fifth fundamental is Embody a Leader's Heart.

While you want all members of your team to demonstrate good character—honesty, integrity, respect, and more—leaders must possess some additional traits—Hungering for Wisdom, Expecting the Best, Accepting Responsibility, Responding with Courage, and Thinking Others First—which we'll outline in the subsequent chapters.

Remember, the single biggest factor that will determine your leadership efficacy, influence, and impact is your heart. Start with the heart as you seek uncommon greatness!

If your heart is not right, no one cares about your skills.

Hunger for Wisdom

The great leaders of today will never be the thriving leaders of tomorrow if they neglect to Hunger for Wisdom. The good news is, wisdom can be forged in the heart of a leader, and the best leaders intentionally pursue it.

This involves a few key tactics: first and foremost being a commitment to lifelong learning. Once committed, leaders must create a plan, knowing wisdom will not be stumbled upon. This involves pursuing chances to learn every day, and— when they do—paying it forward to humbly help others realize there is always more to learn.

As a leader, your capacity to grow—and, ultimately, lead—is determined by your capacity to hunger for wisdom!

Question to Consider

What have you learned recently that you could share with others?

WISDOM ENABLES BETTER DECISIONS.

LEADERS WHO HUNGER FOR WISDOM HUMBLY ADMIT THEY ALWAYS HAVE MORE TO LEARN.

YOUR CAPACITY TO GROW DETERMINES YOUR CAPACITY TO LEAD.

ACTIVATION IDEAS TO

Hunger for Wisdom

☐ **Commit to Lifelong Learning**

STUDY UP: Think of a leader you admire who champions the tactic of being a lifelong learner. This can be someone you personally know, or a leader you can research from afar. What can you learn about their commitment to growth?

DATE COMPLETED: _____

☐ **Create a Plan**

ANNUAL PLAN: You can do a weekly, monthly, annual, or five-year plan. We recommend a one-year time horizon. Make your annual plan specific, focused, individualized, and review it often. Visit LeadEveryDay.com/My Plan to Grow for additional resources.

DATE COMPLETED: _____

☐ Learn Every Day

DAILY REFLECTION: For the next two weeks, at the end of every day ask yourself, "What did I learn today?" Write down your response. Ask yourself what was different on the days you did and the days you did not. My guess is that with less effort than you probably expect, you can embrace the personal leadership discipline to learn something new every day.

DATE COMPLETED: _____

☐ Pay It Forward

LEARNING PRESENTATION: Set aside a meeting in the next thirty days to share something you're learning. Encourage sign-ups for subsequent meetings and make it a monthly event.

DATE COMPLETED: _____

Expect the Best

There is an optimistic tone we expect from leaders we choose to follow. After all, who would opt to embrace a leader whose vision of the future is one painted as worse than today? Great leaders **Expect the Best** by understanding the challenges of the day while simultaneously seeing the world as it could be, with a confidence in their power to make it so.

While embracing the truth of their current realities, leaders who expect the best start with learning to be optimistic, remembering wins to know that an unknown future isn't as daunting as it may seem because of success in the past. Plus, optimistic leaders are more likely to express gratitude, which creates a flywheel-like cycle to greatness!

Question to Consider

Would others consider me
to be an optimistic person?

**WE EXPECT OPTIMISM FROM
LEADERS WE CHOOSE TO FOLLOW.**

**LEADERS WHO EXPECT THE BEST
SEE THE WORLD AS IT COULD BE AND
BELIEVE THEY CAN MAKE IT SO.**

OPTIMISM CAN BE LEARNED.

Expect the Best

☐ Learn to Be Optimistic

POSITIVITY DIGEST: Seek out positive news sources to get your daily news. (A quick online search of "positive news outlets" will give you some options.) See how absorbing this to start your day will transform your mindset.

DATE COMPLETED: _____

☐ Remember Your Wins

SMALL WINS: Get out a piece of computer paper and list as many small past wins as you can think of in ten minutes. This can be anything from hiring a talented new team member to solving a festering problem. Keep this list saved and visible.

DATE COMPLETED: _____

☐ Express Gratitude

DAILY DUTY: Make it a point to express gratitude to someone at work every day. Ensure your actions are authentic, your words are sincere, and the level of acknowledgment is appropriate for the task completed.

DATE COMPLETED: _____

Accept Responsibility

At its core, Accepting Responsibility is about a leader's willingness to be accountable for his or her actions and the actions of those they lead.

This starts with doing their job, and avoiding getting lost in the trenches or bogged down in busyness. Secondly, they admit their mistakes. After all, mistakes are inevitable; how you handle them is your choice. And, finally, leaders who accept responsibility know when to shine the light on others. They give praise freely, and avoid accepting all the credit when things go right.

If you're the leader, you are accountable for results—good and bad. By developing the habit of accepting responsibility, you will encourage others to confidently do the same.

Question to Consider

When is a time you failed to accept responsibility appropriately, and how did/can you rectify it?

ACCEPTING RESPONSIBILITY IS A TEST OF LEADERSHIP CHARACTER WHEN THINGS GO WRONG.

LEADERS ARE RESPONSIBLE FOR RESULTS—GOOD AND BAD.

LEADERS TAKE THE BLAME AND SHARE THE CREDIT.

Accept Responsibility

☐ **Do Your Job**

LOOK BACK: Look back at your last week. How much of your time did you invest doing your job?

DATE COMPLETED: _____

☐ **Admit Your Mistakes**

MIRROR GREATNESS: Think of a leader you admire who does an exemplary job of admitting their mistakes. Take notes on how you can live out their best practices in your life and leadership.

DATE COMPLETED: _____

☐ **Give Praise Freely**

WEEKLY SPOTLIGHT: Find someone on your team or in your organization you can recognize this week. Make the moment personal and specific, and work to make this type of behavior second nature—or, at least, have it happen weekly.

DATE COMPLETED: _____

Respond with Courage

Responding with Courage is the habit that enables leaders to get things done.

Fortunately, becoming courageous is within the grasp of any leader. It all starts with acknowledging your fears. After all, the real heroes aren't those without fear; they are the ones who move beyond them. As you move past your fears and work to strengthen your courage, be patient. Even one small courageous action per day, week, or month will work the muscle, until you are stronger and braver.

As you take these steps, you may encounter failure. Courageous leaders fail forward, learning from their mistakes and persevering to the finish line.

Strengthening your courage muscle may be tough, but what's even tougher is choosing complacency. Are you ready to respond with courage?

Question to Consider

What is your biggest leadership fear and how have/will you overcome it?

COURAGE ENABLES LEADERS TO GET THINGS DONE.

COURAGEOUS LEADERS PERSEVERE TO THE FINISH.

COURAGE CAN BE STRENGTHENED.

Respond with Courage

☐ Acknowledge Your Fears

HEAD-ON: Make two lists. First, put down things you are afraid of in life (e.g., public speaking, death, fear of failure, etc.). Next, look at your calendar for the next week. Are there any upcoming activities that stir fear or anxiety on your schedule (e.g., a presentation to the board, a hard conversation with an employee, etc.)? Armed with these two lists, ask yourself: *"What can I do to reduce or at least mitigate these fears?"*

DATE COMPLETED: _____

☐ Fail Forward

FAILURE REFLECTION: On your most recent failure you can identify, or for the next one to happen, engage in a three-step process afterward: First, name the failure. Second, identify root causes. And, third, ruminate on what you learned.

DATE COMPLETED: _____

☐ **Stretch Yourself**

DECIDE WHAT: If you want to jump start your efforts to be more courageous, or just accelerate your development, try something that will stretch you. It doesn't have to be a mountain or a race. Go back to school, take the bar, start a nonprofit, or launch a start-up as a side hustle. Decide what you're going to do and the first step to help you

DATE COMPLETED: _____

Think Others First

The ability to **Think Others First** is not only the most important of the five habits to embody a leader's heart—it is truly foundational to the pursuit of uncommon greatness.

The choice to serve others is innately challenging but will inevitably become easier as you learn the tactics.

First, think of how you can add value to those you lead. Adding value can be done in endless ways, from encouraging to empathizing to coaching someone, and more. Second, listen to understand. Thinking others first becomes exceedingly difficult if we cannot hear them. And lastly, lead with empathy.

Are you a true influence or merely a leader in title? The ability to think others first may be the differentiator.

Question to Consider

Am I serving others
before considering myself?

Things to Remember

**THINKING OTHERS FIRST IS
FOUNDATIONAL TO THE PURSUIT
OF UNCOMMON GREATNESS.**

**THINKING OTHERS FIRST
MAY NOT COME NATURALLY.**

**SERVING REQUIRES ADDING
VALUE, LISTENING, AND EMPATHY.**

Think
Others First

☐ ## Add Value

EVERYONE MATTERS: For the next week, try to add value to everyone you meet. How did it go? How did you feel? How did others react? Please email your experience to Mark@LeadEveryDay.com.

DATE COMPLETED: _____

☐ ## Listen to Understand

LISTENING FEEDBACK: If the people you lead were asked to rate your listening, what would they say? You may want to ask them. Slip the question into your next five 1:1s.

DATE COMPLETED: _____

☐ **Lead with Empathy**

ECHO CHAMBER: The next conversation you engage in that requires empathy, practice active listening by repeating what the other person is saying. There is something comforting in knowing we are heard, and this is a key step in demonstrating empathy.

DATE COMPLETED: _____

Next
Steps

You have made it this far! You have discovered the keys to achieving uncommon greatness. If you want to leave a legacy that lasts, our encouragement to you is to **SERVE**:

- ◻ **S**ee the Future

- ◻ **E**ngage and Develop Others

- ◻ **R**einvent Continuously

- ◻ **V**alue Results and Relationships

- ◻ **E**mbody a Leader's Heart

The idea of a leader aiming to SERVE has always been, well, uncommon. However, the uncommon are usually the boundary-breakers. The uncommon are the go-getters. The uncommon are the world-changers! Are you ready to command the attention of the world as you SERVE?

If you haven't done so yet, we suggest reading the book *Uncommon Greatness*, as well as keeping the *Uncommon Greatness Quick Start Guide* close at hand. To continue the process of continual growth, we recommend supplementing the information you've learned here by reading the Additional Resources found in the subsequent pages and available at LeadEveryDay.com. Altogether, they will lead you to a life of greatness.

ENJOY THE JOURNEY!

Lead Every Day

Become a Better Leader

 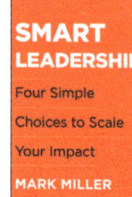 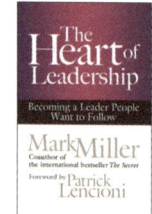

Improve Team Performance

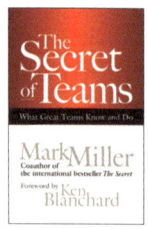 

Strengthen Your Organization

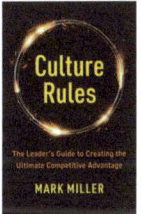

Accelerate Your Success

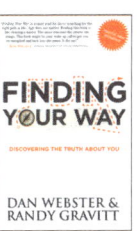

CONTACT THE

Authors

MARK MILLER

Co-Founder
Lead Every Day

EMAIL: mark@leadeveryday.com

WEB: leadeveryday.com

X: @markmillerleads

INSTAGRAM: @leadeveryday

YOUTUBE: @Lead_Every_Day

RANDY GRAVITT

CEO and Co-Founder
Lead Every Day

EMAIL: randy@leadeveryday.com

WEB: leadeveryday.com

X: @randygravitt

INSTAGRAM: @leadeveryday

YOUTUBE: @Lead_Every_Day

FOR LEADERSHIP COACHING OR TRAINING
EMAIL INFO@LEADEVERYDAY.COM